P9-DDP-523

Bernie Williams

Quiet Superstar

by
Kevin Kernan

SPORTS PUBLISHING INC.
www.SportsPublishingInc.com

Book design: Michelle R. Dressen, Susan M. McKinney
Cover design: Scot Muncaster
Photos: *The Associated Press* and the Columbus Clippers

ISBN: 1-58261-004-5
Library of Congress Catalog Card Number: 99-61956

SPORTS PUBLISHING INC.
SportsPublishingInc.com

Printed in the United States.

CONTENTS

Bernie was an important part of the 1998 Yankees team that won an incredible 125 games. (AP/Wide World Photos)

Time to Think

This walk in center field was different than all others Bernie Williams had taken in his life.

His New York Yankees had just completed a four-game sweep of the San Diego Padres to capture the Yankees' 24th World Series championship. At the age of 30, Bernie was on top of the baseball world. He was batting fourth and playing center field for the team with the best record in major league history. The Yankees had won an incredible 125 games in 1998 and lost only 50. Opposing managers referred to him as the "heart and soul" of the team, the best all-round player on the team with the best record of all time.

Most of Bernie's teammates were in the visiting clubhouse at Qualcomm Stadium, in San Diego, celebrating their victory. They had been chanting, "Straw-man, Straw-man" in honor of beloved teammate Darryl Strawberry, who was back home in New Jersey battling cancer. The celebration had spilled onto the infield, where a number of key Yankees—Paul O'Neill, David Wells and Tino Martinez —were talking with reporters from around the country.

Bernie, a gentle and thoughtful man, decided this was the best time to take a walk back to where he belonged, to center field. He wanted to get away from the media, even away from his teammates. So with his wife Waleska at his side, Bernie headed to the green grass of center on a perfect San Diego night.

Out in the outfield, Bernie collapsed on the grass and looked into the night sky, much like when he was a child growing up in Puerto Rico. As a boy, he would lie on the beach, taking in the soft breezes and dreaming about his future.

"That was partly a sigh of relief but also it was taking a deep breath before everything started up," Waleska said of that moment.

Even though his dreams had come true, Bernie knew he would be facing the most difficult time of his professional life over the next month. After 14 years in the Yankee organization, Bernie became a free agent when the last out of the World Series was made. He was free to choose any team in the base-ball universe. His timing was perfect. His value was never higher as a ballplayer, but did he want to leave New York? Would this be his last game as a Yankee? If so, Bernie would leave on top. During the 1998 season, the switch-hitter became the first player in

Bernie watches a St. John's-Duke basketball game with his son, Bernie Alexander. (AP/Wide World Photos)

major league history to win a batting title, a Gold Glove and World Championship all in the same year!

Decisions had to be made that would deeply affect his life and the lives of his wife and three young children, Bernie Alexander, 8, Beatrice, 4, and three-year-old Bianca. He was at the crossroads of his life. Bernie, who also is a wonderful musician, knew he needed to find harmony in his baseball life and family. He picked himself up and walked with Waleska around center field.

"So much was going through my mind, I just had to take it all in," he said.

Bernie is not your typical athlete. He does not put himself on a pedestal. "I think for the most part, people see professional athletes as people that nothing can happen to them, that they are untouchable, that nothing can get to them," he explained. "That they are Superman. We're as human as the next guy. We have to eat. We have to sleep. We cry sometimes, we laugh sometimes. We just have some ability that most people don't have and we try to make the most out of it."

Several thousand Yankee fans stayed in the stadium, part of the crowd of 65,427, the largest crowd to ever watch a baseball game in San Diego. Those fans made their way behind the Yankee dugout, cheering their heroes. They began chanting, "Bernie Please Stay" and he gave the fans a wave.

The Arizona Diamondbacks were rumored to be willing to make Bernie the richest player in baseball, offering $100 million, more money than Bernie ever dreamed about making. But the Diamondbacks were a young team, with little hope of making it to the playoffs. Should he stay with a contender and jump to the Red Sox, who were willing to pay him the same kind of money as the Diamondbacks? The Red Sox, though, were the Yankees' most hated rival and Bernie did not know if he would fit into that team or that city.

Bernie and Waleska circled center field as Louie Armstrong's classic, "What A Wonderful World," played on the stadium sound system. The two kissed and held hands like high school sweethearts. Whatever was going to happen, it was clear at that moment that Bernie and Waleska would make this decision together.

Bernie was born in the Bronx but grew up in Puerto Rico. (AP/Wide World Photos)

2

Setting the Foundation

Bernie's parents, Rufina and Bernabe Williams Sr., made certain their two sons, Bernabe and Hiram, grew up with a well-rounded education. Sports were only a part of young Bernie's life, growing up Puerto Rico. Music, education and culture also played defining roles.

When Bernie was one year old and his younger brother Hiram was a newborn, the family moved from the Bronx to their native Puerto Rico. Bernabe gave up his job in the Merchant Marine to move to Puerto Rico so he could spend more time with his sons. Bernie's mother went to school at the university to earn her Master's degree. She became a teacher and high school principal. Bernabe got a job as a security guard at the school. They made college a family experience. Rufina would go to her classes while the children would go to their school. At night Bernie and Hiram would play in the university's gym and swimming pool with their father.

They were a loving family and the two boys were the light of their parents' life. "We put everything aside in life to make them first," said Rufina. The parents spent many hours opening the worlds of music, culture and sports to their sons and Bernabe would play baseball with his sons every day.

"Education was first," Rufina said. "I tell them so that he remembers for the rest of his life. Because if you don't have a good education, it's really hard to live." Now, Bernie and Waleska tell the same thing to their children.

Like most mothers, Rufina wanted her boys to play sports because she thought they were watching too much television. This was before video games became an everyday part of a child's life.

Just as the parents wanted to unlock the athleticism in their children, they wanted to unlock the music in their sons, too. As soon as Bernie could walk, he was dancing when his father played the guitar. Music would play a key role in Bernie's life. As a child Bernie never thought he would someday play for the Yankees. His dreams revolved around music.

"Not in my wildest dreams did I think about getting to the big leagues," he said. "I wasn't even a good player."

Bernie loved baseball and had fond memories of attending clinics conducted by major league players such as Dickie Thon and Carmelo Martinez. Years later, Bernie would be happy to do the same for children of another generation. Bernie was a good student and a good musician. At the age of eight he started to play the guitar. He fell in love with the instrument and with classical music. He continued to study music and graduated from Escuela Libre de Musica High School in San Juan. Bernie likes all kind of music. "The truth is I like classical," he says, "and I listen to a lot of jazz, but playing blues is what I like best."

At the age of 16 Bernie had to make a big decision. Baseball scouts loved his potential and he loved music. Should he sign with the Yankees, should he continue his education so he could someday become a doctor, or should he go on to study music? His mother thought the odds of her son making it to the majors were about 100,000 to one.

The long hours that his parents Rufina and Bernabe worked with their children had paid off and Bernie could go in any direction in life that he chose. Bernie decided to give baseball a chance.

"Man, it was a hard choice," Bernie said. "At the time, 16 years old, what are the odds of me making it to the big leagues? Not good. Making it as a musician would have probably been harder."

Bernie thought over and over about the road he should travel. "The safest thing was to go to college and get a degree," he said. He did not travel down the safe road. Bernie chose baseball, as did his childhood teammate and current friend and rival, slugger Juan Gonzalez of the Texas Rangers.

To this day, the music still plays inside of Bernie, though. He admires the great guitarists as much as he admires a great athlete. "Talk about pressure," he said, "that's pressure."

In many ways, Bernie says playing the guitar in front of an audience is a lot like facing Roger Clemens in front of a roaring crowd. Hitting the perfect pitch is like hitting all the right notes.

"When I listen to Pat Metheney or Van Halen, I know how hard it is getting that sound perfect," he says. "If you play live, you have just one chance to get it right, especially if you're playing something as measured as classical music." The work ethic for being an athlete and a musician are the same, he said. "You don't leave it wrong till you get it right," he once explained.

He remembered once playing a "Brazilian piece," at school when he was 15. Halfway through he "blanked out" and forgot the music. He ran off the stage crying.

Bernie knew there would be times that he would "blank out" in baseball and make mistakes. There would even be times that he would want to run away, but he had made a decision that he would give baseball his best shot. He was not going to turn back.

3

A Young Colt

The night was warm late in the spring of 1985 when baseball writer George King was watching an amateur game in Ceppa Field in Meridan, Connecticut. A team from a baseball academy was playing and King couldn't help but notice one lanky player. He made a mental note of the 15-year-old player's name, Bernie Williams.

"He was real raw but was hitting bullets," King recalled. "Without a doubt, he was the best amateur player I saw that year."

A few months later when he turned 16, Bernie was signed by Yankees scout Fred Ferreiro after being recommended by Roberto Rivera.

There were to be many years of apprenticeship for Bernie. The lessons learned in music made him a better ballplayer. Just as Bernie knew he had to practice the guitar as a classical musician, he had to practice baseball, including all the mental and physical aspects of the game. His baseball studies at times seemed never-ending. It took a seven-year apprenticeship before Bernie made it to the major leagues to stay.

When he became a professional ballplayer Bernie did not know what to expect, but he knew he was going to try his hardest. "I had so much to learn," he said.

The Yankees can be the most impatient of organizations, but after years of trading away future stars like Fred McGriff, who was originally drafted by the Yankees, the club was determined to give their young "star" players like Bernie plenty of time to learn.

Bernie's first year of professional baseball was at Sarasota, Florida in the Gulf Coast League in 1986. He showed signs early that he would be a special player. In that first season, it was his speed that made Bernie different than the rest of the players in that rookie league. He led the league in runs scored with 45, but also was caught stealing more than any other player. He could run fast, but he really had no idea where he was going or how to get a jump on a pitcher to steal a base.

In his minor league journey, his inexperience sometimes set him back. On July 14, 1988, Bernie ran into the wall and broke his right wrist. His season was over. Despite that injury, the Yankees bumped Bernie up two levels at the start of the next season, putting him at Triple A Columbus, Ohio.

Bernie played for the Triple A Columbus Clippers in 1989, 1991 and 1992. (Columbus Clippers)

Not surprisingly, he struggled. Bernie batted only .216 with two home runs and 16 RBI in the first 50 games. He was then demoted to Double A Albany, New York, where he played the rest of the year. His numbers weren't spectacular, but he was beginning to show signs of lightning-like power. He was becoming a man.

Not wanting to make the same mistake the next year, the Yankees started Bernie in Albany and he stayed the entire season. By the end of the year he was rated the second-best prospect in the Eastern League after leading the league in runs, stolen bases and walks. He was being groomed as the leadoff hitter of the Yankees. He could field and throw and he had power, yet knew when to take a walk.

Bernie was frustrated, though. He thought he should have been promoted to Columbus. Deeply upset, he called home, much in the same manner another Yankee farmhand center fielder did 40 years earlier. On that call, Mickey Mantle's dad convinced his son to stay. On this call, Bernie Williams' mom, Rufina, convinced her son not to pack his bags and come home to Puerto Rico.

"I was supposed to go to Triple A," Bernie said of that difficult time. "And for some reason the Yankees decided not to rush me. I was about to give it up. I called my mom and told her I wanted to go to college and play my guitar. But she said, 'No, you're not going to quit.'"

Those words and that support was all Bernie needed to hear. Moms do know best. By the next season, Bernie not only was selected to the Triple A All-Star team, he was in Yankee Stadium the first week of July. His dream of making the majors had come true.

CHAPTER FOUR

Tough Times

Some ballplayers are from the old school. That is, they like to yell, cuss and chew tobacco. Bernie does not curse and he does not chew tobacco. He approaches baseball with the same approach as his music. Because of that calm approach he was misread by some. There were players and coaches who thought Bernie was not tough enough to make it in the major leagues. They said he looked afraid, like a deer caught in the headlights. They nicknamed him Bambi.

***Bernie worked hard during Spring Training in 1998.
(AP/Wide World Photos)***

During his first 85 games in the majors in 1991, Bernie hit only .238. On Aug. 21 in Kansas City he struck out all five times he batted, becoming the first Yankee position player ever to strike out five times in one game. On June 25, 1934, a pitcher named Johnny Broaca also struck out five times, but, at least, he was a pitcher. These were tough times for Bernie.

After starting the next season on the major league roster, he was sent back to Columbus. On July 31, 1992, he returned to the majors for good. Bernie was the Yankees' center fielder of the present and future because the team traded the incumbent, Roberto Kelly, after the 1992 season.

A veteran player named Mel Hall often made fun of Bernie's play, especially the way Bernie ran the bases. Because of his lack of experience, Bernie was sometimes timid on the base paths, afraid to make a mistake. He did not take full advantage of his ability to run fast. Hall used to shout across the

Yankee clubhouse to embarrass Bernie, saying, "How do you score Bernie from first base? Hit a triple."

Such comments upset Bernie and he would storm out of the clubhouse. Bernie would never openly criticize a teammate and could not understand why he was being criticized. "I think Mel used to intimidate Bernie," former Yankee coach Clete Boyer once told a reporter. "Mel was always agitating Bernie. Bernie was scared to death of Mel."

In professional baseball, players are easily labeled. A scout can write a negative report on a young player and those words can stick with the player for years, until he can prove them wrong. Bernie was labeled early as the "sensitive, artist type." In the macho world of major league baseball, that was one way of saying he wasn't tough enough. In 1992, Bernie batted .280 in 62 games.

Hall was gone from the Yankees by 1993 and Bernie began to show he was ready for the challenge of becoming a major league star. Coaches soon took notice. "He looks more sure of himself," Boyer said at the time. "He was timid, but it looks like he's ready to blossom. I think he feels like he belongs now."

The Yankee manager was Buck Showalter, now the manager of the Arizona Diamondbacks. Showalter tried to toughen Bernie by having him train in afternoon spring training sessions with mostly minor leaguers in 1993, even though Bernie was the Yankees' starting center fielder. It seemed that some people wanted to change Bernie's personality, make him something that he was not. Bernie changed his game, becoming more physical, more tough, but he did not change who he was. Today he remains the same soft-spoken, kindhearted person that his parents raised him to be.

When people said Williams couldn't play a physical center field, he proved them wrong by learning to dive and punish his body. His bruises

Bernie is tagged out at home by Seattle Mariners catcher Chris Widger. (AP/Wide World Photos)

became badges of honor. "I like surprising people," Bernie said. "They thought I couldn't play that way and I knew I could. You have to take it as a challenge."

The 1993 season was Bernie's first full season in the majors. He started the year hitting leadoff, but struggled, hitting just .239 through the All-Star break. He moved back to sixth in the lineup and batted .310 the rest of the year. The only thing that stopped Bernie in 1994 was the strike. The baseball season ended prematurely but Bernie put up solid numbers, batting .289 with 12 homers and 57 RBI with 16 stolen bases in 25 attempts over 108 games.

Bernie did not know it at the time, but he was becoming a quiet star. In just two years he would blossom into one of the best all-around players in baseball.

*Bernie makes a diving catch to save a base hit.
(AP/Wide World Photos)*

5

Breaking Out

The Yankees had not been to the post-season since 1981, but made it to the playoffs in 1995 and Bernie's performance was a big reason for their success. Mickey Mantle, the last great Yankee center fielder, died that summer as Bernie came into his own, batting .307, one point higher than Mantle batted 30 years earlier, with 18 home runs and 82 RBI, all career highs. In addition, Bernie produced nine triples, the most by a Yankee in 13 years. He also proved to be a durable player, missing only two starts in center field.

Bernie with Bianca, his youngest child, in 1996. (AP/Wide World Photos)

Late in the season, on Sept. 15, Bernie was unable to fly to Puerto Rico because of a hurricane and was not present for the birth of his daughter Bianca. Then the Yankees wanted Bernie to remain with the team and he did. He did not fly home until 10 days later. He learned from that point on that family came first.

As Bernie matured, so did his game. In the divisional playoffs the Yankees lost to Seattle in five games, including all three games in Seattle. Despite the loss, Bernie had put the baseball world on notice that he was a budding superstar. In a 7-4 defeat in Game 3, Bernie became the first player in postseason history to hit a home run from both sides of the plate in the same game. He batted .429 in the series. That was a sign of things to come because in 1996, Bernie and the Yankees were unstoppable.

The success of the World Champion 1996 Yankees can be attributed to many factors. One was the hiring of Joe Torre as manager to replace Showalter. Torre is extremely patient, the kind of manager who brings out the best in young players, and he quickly became a Bernie backer. Even when criticizing, Torre knew how to do it in such a way to build a player's confidence.

"Now if he's tentative," Torre said of Bernie, who hit .305 that season with 29 homers and 102 RBI, the most homers by a Yankee center fielder in 24 years, "it's only because he's feeling his way, and he's still trying to learn things. He's a very confident player, and he's getting more confident all the time."

Bernie admitted he was more relaxed with Torre in charge, but that he loved the pressure of playing in pinstripes. "It's electrifying," he said. "Especially on the New York stage."

Bernie's music remained important to him. That was a stage he loved, too. At Yankee Stadium he would sometimes scoot off to an empty storeroom to play his guitar, away from the noise of the clubhouse. He also played guitar at a famous New York club called The Bottom Line.

Bernie remained the shy and silent star, though. "I'm still learning," he said. "I still haven't reached my peak. I hope the best years of my career are ahead of me."

Torre knew that to be true, too, and worked with Bernie not to get so down on himself when things went bad. Torre said that Bernie's love of the game would make him a star.

During the final weekend of the regular season, the Yankees had already clinched the American League East title. They were at Fenway Park in Boston, which has the famous Green Monster, the wall in left field that runs all the way to center, creating all kinds of difficult plays for the left and center fielders. It was the kind of weekend when a lesser

Bernie batted .467 against the Rangers in the 1996 American League Division Series. (AP/Wide World Photos)

player might take himself out of the lineup so he could be well-rested for the playoffs.

Torre gave Bernie the option of not playing that series. Bernie, who always looks you straight in the eye when he wants to make a point, would not agree to sit. He told his manager: "This is when you want to be playing. This is when you get ready."

Bernie was ready to break out in the playoffs. He did in a huge way, pounding the Rangers' pitchers for a .467 average and three homers in the divisional series victory. In the clinching Game 4, he sparked the Yankees to a comeback victory by blasting two home runs, one right-handed, one left, duplicating his major league first of a year earlier. His old buddy Juan Gonzalez crushed five homers in the series for the Rangers but Bernie's performance led the Yankees to victory.

Bernie continued his assault against the Orioles in the American League Championship Series, hitting .474 with two homers and six RBI, including the game-winning homer to lead off the bottom of the 11th in Game 1 as the Yankees completed their fourth straight come-from-behind win. The team was coming together with everything on the line and Bernie was leading the way. No one was questioning his toughness now.

After losing Game 2, the Yankees rallied to win the pivotal third game, 5-2, scoring four times in the top of the eighth with Bernie knocking in the tying run and scoring the winner. He crushed a two-run blast in the first inning of the Yankees' 8-4 Game 4 victory. Marveled Orioles manager Davey Johnson, "I don't know how you can get him out."

Bernie had made his mark and won MVP honors for the series. "He's quiet, laid back, but carries a big stick," said Bernie's teammate Tim Raines.

That season Bernie also kept his word about family coming first. He flew home in June when his son Bernie Alexander developed a serious ear infection that required surgery.

"After that series he had against Baltimore," teammate Paul O'Neill said, "some people would have been out partying in Manhattan, but Bernie wanted to go home to his wife and kids. That's the way Bernie is."

Bernie is always working hard to succeed, putting in the extra effort necessary in practice. (AP/Wide World Photos)

A Sense of History

The glory the Yankees brought back to the Bronx in 1996 was not to be repeated the following year. Bernie made the All-Star team for the first time as he finished fourth in the league with a .328 average, added 21 homers and 100 RBI. Lack of clutch play haunted the Yankees in their division series matchups against Cleveland. The success that Bernie had the previous year disappeared and he was the Yankee who made the final out in the team's final game of the year, a 4-3 loss at Jacobs Field.

Bernie talks with Yankees owner George Steinbrenner.
(AP/Wide World Photos)

Bernie thought he had let his whole team down. He had just two hits in 17 at-bats in the series, a .118 average. He was going into his free agent contract year and there were those in the organization who thought he would not be able to handle the pressure that would place on him. It's never easy to face an uncertain future, and it's even tougher when you work for an owner like Yankees boss George Steinbrenner, who demands the best from all his players. For 15 minutes Bernie sat at his locker with his head down. Teammates stopped by to offer encouragement, but he still felt the weight of the world on his shoulders as he walked out of the clubhouse that night.

Bernie promised himself that in 1998 he would work even harder to succeed. "Bernie never does anything out of character," said Yankee first baseman Tino Martinez, one of Bernie's best friends. "Whether he's struggling or going great, he always keeps the same mind-set."

That kind of self-discipline is lacking in many of today's athletes. Bernie was certain he would find his rhythm again even though the pressure would be intense. The pressure starts at the top.

Steinbrenner has owned the Yankees for 25 years. He once criticized another talented player for not producing in the post-season, referring to Dave Winfield as "Mr. May." "Baseball is all about pressure and how you handle it," Bernie said. "If you play in New York, you have to face adversity and different challenges. If you want to play here, you have to handle that."

The pressure made Bernie a better player and so did the Yankees' rich history. Tradition is something Bernie deeply respects. That's why he is overwhelmed sometimes when he thinks about the great Yankee center fielders that have gone before him, including Mantle and Joe DiMaggio. Center field at Yankee Stadium is the most hallowed ground in baseball and Monument Park in left-center is a daily reminder to Bernie how special it is to be a Yankee.

"I tend to think about tradition a lot more than I used to," Bernie said before the season. "I'm constantly hearing about it. You see those monuments behind the outfield wall and say, 'Wow!' Sometimes it hits me during batting practice or when I walk around out there after the season is over."

When Bernie is in center, he can almost feel the spirit of the Yankee greats. "It doesn't feel like ancient history when you're standing in the same spot where those other guys stood."

The Yankees earned their place in baseball history in 1998, winning 114 games in the regular season, then cruising thought the playoffs, beating the Rangers in three straight and topping the Indians in six games in the critical rematch in the American League playoffs. The crowning glory to the season came in the World Series, when they swept the Padres in four games.

Bernie waves to the crowd after the announcement that he won the 1998 American League batting title. (AP/Wide World Photos)

When the playoffs began there were great expectations for Bernie but he did not get a hit in the division sweep of the Rangers, going 0-for-11. "I'm getting close to finding my stroke," he promised.

Bernie did just that in the ALCS as he led the Yankees with a .381 average. In 11 ALCS games over his career, Bernie has a .425 average. In the World Series, Bernie's home run in Game 2 was his only hit, but that two-run blast put the game out of reach and in the deciding Game 4, he knocked in the game-winner.

Throughout the year, Bernie was at the center of everything. He won his first batting title with a .339 mark, edging Boston's Mo Vaughn on the last day of the season. He became the eighth Yankee to lead the league, joining greats such as Babe Ruth, Lou Gehrig and Mantle. "It's such a great feeling to add your name to the list of players who have accomplished that," he said.

Bernie was named to the All-Star team for the second time. He also won his second Gold Glove, awarded to the best defensive player at each position. During the season there were many individual highlights, including his 4-for-5 performance with a game-winning homer in the bottom of the ninth to beat Texas on Aug. 16, the 50th anniversary of Ruth's death. He did not hit a home run until his 119th at-bat of the season, but finished with 26 homers and 97 RBI.

"I think there was more pressure for me to perform this year than any other year," Bernie said when it was all over. "It's been a grind, but it's been a great year."

Big Decision, Big Payoff

The moment the World Series ended, everyone in New York wanted an answer to the Big Question. Would the Yankees re-sign Bernie?

The Yankees were doing their best to convince the public that Albert Belle would be a wonderful addition if Bernie demanded too much money. There was no doubting Belle's baseball talents. He was a home run and RBI machine, second in both categories in the American League in 1998 with 49 home runs and 152 RBI. Belle, though, was a player who did not get along with the media and has had a number of embarrassing situations during his career. With the spotlight on him in New York, he could easily become an unpopular player. Bernie, meanwhile, was looked upon as class on and off the field and was especially popular with New York's large Latin community because of his many good deeds.

In November, Torre went to Belle's home in Arizona, played golf with the slugger and had dinner with him. He made it sound like the Yankees were truly going to sign Belle. "I'm very confident, he would fit in here," Torre said.

Despite those kind words about Belle, everyone knew how Torre felt about Bernie. "The person (Bernie) reminds me of most is Arthur Ashe," Torre once said. "You see it the way he carries himself. He's quiet, but he has a quiet dignity."

It was that dignity that made Bernie look away from the Yankees. He felt his talents were not really appreciated by the Yankees because of past contract disagreements. Bernie knew he would get more money than he had ever dreamed of making with this contract and in his heart he wanted that offer to come from the team that he had played for the last 13 years. He wanted the Yankees to step up to the plate in a big way.

His wife Waleska said the negotiations were difficult. "We didn't know what we'd have to confront, we didn't know how it would affect us and it affected us more than we thought, especially Bernie," she said.

Bernie had trouble eating and sleeping. "He really didn't think he would feel that bad, but it was more than just baseball," Waleska said. "It wasn't just leaving a work place. It was leaving a home— a place where we grew together as a family for eight

After the 1998 season, the Yankees signed Bernie to a new seven-year contract. (AP/Wide World Photos)

years. It was like leaving a part of you. It wasn't just the money we had to consider, we had to consider where our children would settle. ... When we told them that we might be leaving they felt very bad and didn't understand."

Bernie thought his Yankee career was over. "I don't think they have a lot of interest," he said on Nov. 21. "They keep saying, 'He's our top priority,' but when it comes down to it, they just don't show it."

On the day before Thanksgiving, however, the Yankees were able to keep Bernie as he signed a monumental seven-year, $87.5 million contract. Everyone was thrilled. Yankee general manager Brian Cashman had termed the negotiations with Belle, Bernie and Brian Jordan as a round of musical chairs. When the music stopped, he wanted to be certain the Yankees had a chair to sit in. "This is the most comfortable chair we wanted to sit in,"

Bernie wants to finish his career as a Yankee.
(AP/Wide World Photos)

Cashman said of Bernie. "This is the one chair that fits in with everything else. Bernie has proven that."

In the end, Bernie relied on the lessons he had learned as a young boy about the importance of family and friends. The Yankees were his family. It was where Bernie learned to play baseball. From the time he was 16 he was a Yankee and he signed a contract that would keep him a Yankee for the rest of his career. "He is the loudest quiet player in all of baseball," is the way his agent Scott Boras described Bernie's worth to the Yankees in terms of leadership and production inside the clubhouse and on the field.

"I love New York, this is where I wanted to be," Bernie said. "I am very happy that this whole thing is over with. Now I can concentrate on us defending our title."

Bernie and Waleska's friendship with Tino Martinez and his wife Marie also played a part in

The popular Bernie hands a signed baseball to a young fan.
(AP/Wide World Photos)

their final decision. "It became a joke between us that if we would stay, they would have to also," Waleska said. "So we joked that we'd try to get a clause in Bernie's contract that said the Yankees have to re-sign Tino when the time comes."

World Series MVP Scott Brosius called Bernie, "the perfect teammate."

Three days after Bernie signed his contract, he was back in the New York area at a card show. All the fans wished him well and congratulated him on staying. Even if he signed with the Red Sox he said he still would have come to the show. "It would have been kind of strange, kind of awkward, coming here as something other than a Yankee, so soon," he said. "But I'm just glad I didn't have to think about any of that. This is where I'm comfortable. This is where I should be. I wanted to remain a Yankee for the rest of my career. Now I can. It would have been very difficult to say goodbye to a place where we collected so many memories. This is home."

Home at Yankee Stadium. Home in center field.

Bernie, center, celebrates with teammates Chuck Knoblauch, left, and Jorge Posada after another Yankee victory. (AP/Wide World Photos)

Bernie Williams Quick Facts

Full Name:	Bernabe Figueroa Williams
Team:	New York Yankees
Hometown:	Bayamon, Puerto Rico
Position:	Outfielder
Jersey Number:	51
Bats:	Switch-hitter
Throws:	Right
Height:	6-2
Weight:	205 pounds
Birthdate:	September 13, 1968

1998 Highlight: Won American League batting title.

Stats Spotlight: Has averaged 25 home runs and 100 RBI the last three seasons.

Little-known fact: At age 15 Williams was one of the world's top 400-meter runners.

Bernie won the American League batting title in 1998 with a .339 average. (AP/Wide World Photos)

Bernie Williams'
Professional Career

Year	Club	AVG	G	AB	R	H	2B	3B	HR	RBI	BB	SO	SB
1986	Sarasota	.270	61	230	45*	62	5	3	2	25	39	40	33
1987	Ft. Laud.	.155	25	71	11	11	3	0	0	4	18	22	9
	Oneonta	.344	25	93	13	32	4	0	0	15	10	14	9
1988	Prince Wm.	.335*	92	337	72	113	16	7	7	45	65	65	29
1989	Albany	.252	91	314	63	79	11	8	11	42	60	72	26
	Columbus	.216	50	162	21	35	8	1	2	16	25	38	11
1990	Albany	.281	134	466	91*	131	28	5	8	54	98*	97	39*
1991	Columbus	.294	78	306	52	90	14	6	8	37	38	43	9
	Yankees	.238	85	320	43	76	19	4	3	34	48	57	10
1992	Columbus	.306	95	363	68	111	23	9	8	50	52	61	20
	Yankees	.280	62	261	39	73	14	2	5	26	29	36	7
1993	Yankees	.268	139	567	67	152	31	4	12	68	53	106	9
1994	Yankees	.289	108	408	80	118	29	1	12	57	61	54	16
1995	Yankees	.307	144	563	93	173	29	9	18	82	75	98	8
1996	Yankees	.305	143	551	108	168	26	7	29	102	82	72	17
1997	Yankees	.328	129	509	107	167	35	6	21	100	73	80	15
1998	Yankees	.339*	128	499	101	169	30	5	26	97	74	81	15

Minor League Ttls		.284	651	2342	436	664	112	39	46	288	405	452	185
Yankees Totals		.298	938	3678	638	1096	213	38	126	566	495	584	97
Post Season Ttls		**.278**	**38**	**144**	**31**	**40**	**7**	**0**	**9**	**29**	**31**	**30**	**5**

*Denotes League Leader

Bernie's major-league career batting average is .298.
(AP/Wide World Photos)

Career Fielding Statistics

Year	Team	Posn	G	GS	TC	PO	A	E	P	FLD%
1991	Yankees	OF	85	85	238	230	3	5	0	.979
1992	Yankees	OF	62	61	193	187	5	1	2	.995
1993	Yankees	OF	139	139	375	366	5	4	0	.989
1994	Yankees	OF	107	104	287	277	7	3	2	.990
1995	Yankees	OF	144	143	441	432	1	8	0	.982
1996	Yankees	OF	140	140	349	334	10	5	3	.986
1997	Yankees	OF	128	127	274	270	2	2	1	.993
1998	Yankees	OF	123	123	305	298	4	3	1	.990
Fielding Totals			928	922	2462	2394	37	31	9	.987
Post Season Fielding Ttls		38	38	93	93	0	0	0	1.000

1998 AL MVP Voting

Juan Gonzalez	357
Nomar Garciaparra	232
Derek Jeter	180
Mo Vaughn	135
Ken Griffey Jr.	135
Manny Ramirez	127
Bernie Williams	**103**

Third base coach Willie Randolph, left, high-fives Bernie after a home run in Game 2 of the 1998 World Series. (AP/Wide World Photos)

1998 AL BA Leaders

Bernie Williams	**.339**
Mo Vaughn	.337
Albert Belle	.328
Eric Davis	.327
Derek Jeter	.324

Bernie's Big Year

Following is a regular-season game-by-game breakdown of Bernie Williams' 1998 campaign in which he captured the American League batting title with a .339 average.

Date	Opp	AB	R	H	2B	3B	HR	RBI
4/01/98	@Ana	4	1	3	0	0	0	0
4/02/98	@Ana	4	0	0	0	0	0	0
4/04/98	@Oak	4	0	0	0	0	0	0
4/05/98	@Oak	4	1	1	0	0	0	1
4/06/98	@Sea	4	0	0	0	0	0	0
4/07/98	@Sea	4	1	1	1	0	0	1
4/08/98	@Sea	5	0	3	1	0	0	1
4/10/98	OAK	3	4	2	0	0	0	0
4/11/98	OAK	3	0	1	0	0	0	0
4/12/98	OAK	4	1	2	0	0	0	2

Derek Jeter, left, congratulates Bernie after Bernie's home run off Padres pitcher Andy Ashby in the World Series. (AP/Wide World Photos)

Date	Opp	AB	R	H	2B	3B	HR	RBI
4/15/98	ANA	3	0	0	0	0	0	0
4/17/98	@Det	4	1	0	0	0	0	0
4/18/98	@Det	3	1	2	0	0	0	2
4/19/98	@Det	4	0	0	0	0	0	0
4/20/98	@Tor	5	0	0	0	0	0	0
4/21/98	@Tor	4	1	3	1	1	0	1
4/22/98	@Tor	4	2	0	0	0	0	0
4/24/98	DET	2	2	1	0	0	0	1
4/25/98	DET	3	2	1	1	0	0	0
4/27/98	TOR	3	0	1	1	0	0	0

Bernie and pitcher Jeff Nelson, rear, head to the 1998 World Series parade. (AP/Wide World Photos)

Date	Opp	AB	R	H	2B	3B	HR	RBI
4/28/98	TOR	4	1	2	1	1	0	0
4/29/98	SEA	4	1	1	0	0	0	0
4/30/98	SEA	4	1	1	0	0	0	0
5/01/98	@KC	3	0	1	0	0	0	2
5/02/98	@KC	5	3	3	0	0	0	0
5/03/98	@KC	3	0	0	0	0	0	0
5/05/98	@Tex	4	0	1	1	0	0	0
5/06/98	@Tex	5	2	3	0	2	0	0
5/08/98	@Min	5	0	1	0	0	0	1
5/09/98	@Min	4	0	0	0	0	0	0

Bernie, left, and fellow major leaguers Jorge Posada (Yankees, second from left), Ivan Rodriguez (Texas Rangers) and Jose Canseco (Toronto Blue Jays, right) participated in the Carlos Baerga Celebrity Softball Game in Puerto Rico. (AP/Wide World Photos)

Date	Opp	AB	R	H	2B	3B	HR	RBI
5/10/98	@Min	4	0	2	0	0	0	0
5/12/98	KC	2	1	1	0	0	1	2
5/13/98	TEX	3	1	2	0	0	1	4
5/14/98	TEX	5	0	1	1	0	0	0
5/15/98	MIN	4	0	0	0	0	0	0
5/16/98	MIN	4	0	1	1	0	0	0
5/17/98	MIN	3	3	3	2	0	1	1
5/19/98	BAL	4	1	1	0	0	1	3
5/20/98	BAL	2	1	0	0	0	0	0
5/21/98	BAL	4	0	1	0	0	0	1

Date	Opp	AB	R	H	2B	3B	HR	RBI
5/22/98	@Bos	4	1	1	0	0	1	3
5/23/98	@Bos	5	2	2	1	0	0	0
5/24/98	@Bo	5	0	2	1	0	0	1
5/25/98	@ChA	5	2	3	0	0	1	4
5/26/98	@ChA	4	0	1	0	0	0	0
5/27/98	@ChA	5	1	3	0	1	1	5
5/28/98	BOS	2	0	0	0	0	0	0
5/29/98	BOS	4	1	3	1	0	0	0
5/30/98	BOS	4	0	3	0	0	0	0
5/31/98	BOS	5	1	4	0	0	0	0

Date	Opp	AB	R	H	2B	3B	HR	RBI
6/01/98	ChA	4	0	0	0	0	0	0
6/02/98	ChA	4	0	1	0	0	0	0
6/03/98	TB	3	0	0	0	0	0	0
6/04/98	TB	4	1	3	0	0	0	2
6/05/98	FLA	3	1	0	0	0	0	0
6/06/98	FLA	3	1	2	0	0	1	3
6/07/98	FLA	3	1	1	0	0	1	1
6/09/98	@Mon	4	1	2	1	0	1	2
6/10/98	@Mon	3	2	2	1	0	0	0
7/18/98	@Tor	5	3	3	0	0	1	2

***Darryl Strawberry, left, and Bernie celebrate one of
Bernie's 26 home runs in 1998. (AP/Wide World Photos)***

Date	Opp	AB	R	H	2B	3B	HR	RBI
7/19/98	@Tor	3	0	1	0	0	0	1
7/20/98	DET	8	0	3	2	0	0	2
7/21/98	DET	3	0	0	0	0	0	0
7/22/98	DET	4	1	2	0	0	0	0
7/24/98	ChA	4	0	0	0	0	0	0
7/25/98	ChA	4	1	1	0	0	0	0
7/26/98	ChA	4	2	3	1	0	1	2
7/28/98	@Ana	5	1	2	0	0	1	2
7/29/98	@Ana	4	0	0	0	0	0	0
7/30/98	@Ana	2	1	0	0	0	0	0

Date	Opp	AB	R	H	2B	3B	HR	RBI
7/31/98	@Sea	5	0	1	0	0	0	0
8/01/98	@Sea	4	1	2	1	0	0	1
8/02/98	@Sea	3	0	1	0	0	0	0
8/03/98	@Oak	5	1	1	1	0	0	0
8/04/98	@Oak	3	3	2	0	0	0	2
8/04/98	@Oak	5	1	1	0	0	0	0
8/05/98	@Oak	4	0	1	0	0	0	0
8/07/98	KC	4	2	2	0	0	0	2
8/07/98	KC	4	2	2	0	0	1	2
8/08/98	KC	4	1	1	0	0	0	0

Date	Opp	AB	R	H	2B	3B	HR	RBI
8/09/98	KC	3	0	2	0	0	0	2
8/10/98	MIN	4	1	2	0	0	1	1
8/11/98	MIN	4	1	1	0	0	0	0
8/12/98	MIN	5	1	2	0	0	1	1
8/13/98	TEX	3	0	1	0	0	0	0
8/14/98	TEX	3	1	1	0	0	1	1
8/15/98	TEX	3	1	0	0	0	0	1
8/16/98	TEX	5	1	4	0	0	1	1
8/17/98	@KC	5	2	2	0	0	1	2
8/18/98	@KC	6	2	3	1	0	1	1

Date	Opp	AB	R	H	2B	3B	HR	RBI
8/19/98	@Min	4	1	0	0	0	0	0
8/20/98	@Min	5	1	1	1	0	0	0
8/21/98	@Tex	5	0	0	0	0	0	0
8/22/98	@Tex	5	0	4	1	0	0	4
8/23/98	@Tex	5	0	0	0	0	0	0
8/24/98	ANA	4	0	0	0	0	0	0
8/25/98	ANA	5	2	3	1	0	0	1
8/26/98	ANA	4	0	0	0	0	0	0
8/26/98	ANA	4	0	0	0	0	0	0
8/27/98	ANA	4	1	1	1	0	0	1

Date	Opp	AB	R	H	2B	3B	HR	RBI
8/28/98	SEA	3	1	1	0	0	0	1
8/29/98	SEA	5	0	3	1	0	0	4
8/30/98	SEA	4	0	0	0	0	0	0
9/01/98	OAK	4	1	1	0	0	1	2
9/02/98	OAK	4	0	2	1	0	0	0
9/04/98	@ChA	5	3	3	0	0	2	4
9/05/98	@ChA	4	1	3	0	0	0	1
9/06/98	@ChA	4	1	1	0	0	1	3
9/07/98	@Bos	3	0	0	0	0	0	0
9/08/98	@Bos	3	0	1	0	0	0	0

Date	Opp	AB	R	H	2B	3B	HR	RBI
9/09/98	@Bos	3	1	0	0	0	0	0
9/10/98	TOR	3	1	0	0	0	0	0
9/11/98	TOR	4	1	2	1	0	0	0
9/13/98	TOR	4	0	0	0	0	0	0
9/14/98	BOS	4	0	1	0	0	0	0
9/15/98	BOS	4	1	1	0	0	1	1
9/16/98	@TB	2	0	0	0	0	0	0
9/17/98	@TB	4	1	1	0	0	1	1
9/18/98	@Bal	3	0	1	0	0	0	1
9/19/98	@Bal	3	1	2	1	0	0	0

Date	Opp	AB	R	H	2B	3B	HR	RBI
9/20/98	@Bal	5	1	1	0	0	0	0
9/21/98	CLE	4	0	1	0	0	0	0
9/22/98	CLE	4	2	2	0	0	0	0
9/23/98	CLE	4	1	1	0	0	0	0
9/24/98	TB	4	1	1	0	0	0	1
9/25/98	TB	2	0	2	0	0	0	1
9/26/98	TB	4	0	1	0	0	0	0
9/27/98	TB	2	1	2	0	0	0	1
Totals		**499**	**101**	**169**	**30**	**5**	**26**	**97**

Bernie Williams' Career Highlights

- Over the past four seasons (1995-96-97-98), Bernie carries a cumulative batting average of .319 (677 hits in 2,122 at bats).

- During that same four-year period, he has averaged 30 doubles, 6.75 triples, 23.5 home runs and 95.3 RBI per season.

- Over the last three seasons, switch-hitting Bernie has hit .352 against left-handed pitching and .311 against right-handed pitching. His power hitting is much more proficient from the right side however. Bernie has hit 42 home runs right-handed as compared to 34 homers left-handed; he's hit 66 doubles from the right side and only 25 from the left side; and he's accounted for 16 triples as a right-handed batter and just two as a left-handed hitter. Bernie has had nearly twice as many RBI over the last three campaigns as a right-hander, 195 to 104.

- During the last three seasons, Bernie carries a cumulative batting average of .300+ in April (.302), May (.355), June (.342), August (.332) and September (.331), but has batted just .259 during the month of July.

- Versus individual teams, Bernie performs best (over the last three seasons) against the Boston Red Sox (.361), the Texas Rangers (.352), the Baltimore Orioles (.347) and the Oakland Athletics (.345). During that same period, he's struggled the most against the Toronto Blue Jays (.241), the Milwaukee Brewers (.282) and the Anaheim Angels (.291), the only three teams against whom he hitting under .300.

- One of the American League's top centerfielders, Bernie has committed only 31 errors in 2,462 chances. That's a fielding percentage of .987, slightly better than the career percentages posted by former Yankee centerfielders Mickey Mantle (.985) and Joe DiMaggio (.978).

1998 AL Slugging Pct.

Albert Belle	.655
Juan Gonzalez	.630
Ken Griffey Jr.	.611
Manny Ramirez	.599
Carlos Delgado	.592
Mo Vaughn	.591
Nomar Garciaparra	.584
Jim Thome	.584
Eric Davis	.582
Bernie Williams	**.575**

Bernie is part of the Yankees' centerfield tradition that includes such greats as Mickey Mantle, left, and Joe DiMaggio. (AP/Wide World Photos)

1998 AL Triples Leader

Jose Offerman	13	Kenny Lofton	6
Johnny Damon	10	Mike Caruso	6
Randy Winn	9	Otis Nixon	6
Ray Durham	8	Omar Vizquel	6
Derek Jeter	8	Alex Rodriguez	5
Nomar Garciaparra	8	**Bernie Williams**	**5**
Troy O'Leary	8	Migquel Cairo	5
Garret Anderson	7	Mike Cameron	5
Quinton McCracken	7	Rusty Greer	5
Joey Cora	6	Luis Gonzalez	5
Matt Lawton	6	Paul Molitor	5

1998 AL Runs Leaders

1.	Derek Jeter	127
2.	Ray Durham	126
3.	Alex Rodriguez	123
4.	Ken Griffey Jr	120
5.	Chuck Knoblauch	117
20.	**Bernie Williams**	**101**

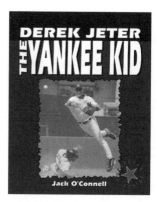

Derek Jeter: The Yankee Kid

Author: Jack O'Connell
ISBN: 1-58261-043-6

In 1996 Derek burst onto the scene as one of the most promising young shortstops to hit the big leagues in a long time. His hitting prowess and ability to turn the double play have definitely fulfilled the early predictions of greatness.

A native of Kalamazoo, MI, Jeter has remained well grounded. He patiently signs autographs and takes time to talk to the young fans who will be eager to read more about him in this book.

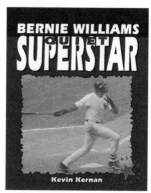

Bernie Williams: Quiet Superstar

Author: Kevin Kernan
ISBN: 1-58261-044-4

Bernie Williams, a guitar-strumming native of Puerto Rico, is not only popular with his teammates, but is considered by top team officials to be the heir to DiMaggio and Mantle fame.

He draws frequent comparisons to Roberto Clemente, perhaps the greatest player ever from Puerto Rico. Like Clemente, Williams is humble, unassuming, and carries himself with quiet dignity. Also like Clemente, he plays with rare determination and a special elegance. He's married, and serves as a role model not only for his three children, but for his young fans here and in Puerto Rico.

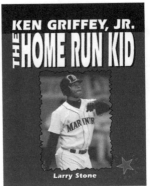

Ken Griffey, Jr.: The Home Run Kid

Author: Larry Stone
ISBN: 1-58261-041-x

Capable of hitting majestic home runs, making breathtaking catches, and speeding around the bases to beat the tag by a split second, Ken Griffey, Jr. is baseball's Michael Jordan. Amazingly, Ken reached the Major Leagues at age 19, made his first All-Star team at 20, and produced his first 100 RBI season at 21.

The son of Ken Griffey, Sr., Ken is part of the only father-son combination to play in the same outfield together in the same game, and, like Barry Bonds, he's a famous son who turned out to be a better player than his father.

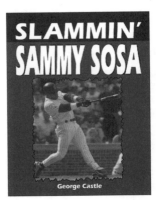

Sammy Sosa: Slammin' Sammy

Author: George Castle
ISBN: 1-58261-029-0

1998 was a break-out year for Sammy as he amassed 66 home runs, led the Chicago Cubs into the playoffs and finished the year with baseball's ultimate individual honor, MVP.

When the national spotlight was shone on Sammy during his home run chase with Mark McGwire, America got to see what a special person he is. His infectious good humor and kind heart have made him a role model across the country.

7920

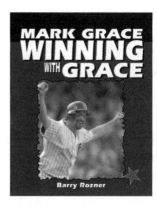

Mark Grace: Winning with Grace

Author: Barry Rozner
ISBN: 1-58261-056-8

This southern California native and San Diego State alumnus has been playing baseball in the windy city for nearly fifteen years. Apparently the cold hasn't affected his game. Mark is an all-around player who can hit to all fields and play great defense.

Mark's outgoing personality has allowed him to evolve into one of Chicago's favorite sons. He is also community minded and some of his favorite charities include the Leukemia Society of America and Easter Seals.

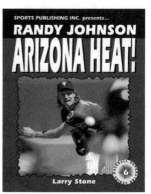

Randy Johnson: Arizona Heat!

Author: Larry Stone
ISBN: 1-58261-042-8

One of the hardest throwing pitchers in the Major Leagues, and, at 6'10" the tallest, the towering figure of Randy Johnson on the mound is an imposing sight which strikes fear into the hearts of even the most determined opposing batters.

Perhaps the most amazing thing about Randy is his consistency in recording strikeouts. He is one of only four pitchers to lead the league in strikeouts for four consecutive seasons. With his recent signing with the Diamondbacks, his career has been rejuvenated and he shows no signs of slowing down.

SUPERSTAR SERIES

Collect Them All!

____ Sandy and Roberto Alomar:
     Baseball Brothers

____ Kevin Brown: Kevin with a "K"

____ Roger Clemens: Rocket Man!

____ Juan Gonzalez: Juan Gone!

____ Mark Grace: Winning With Grace

____ Ken Griffey, Jr.: The Home Run Kid

____ Tony Gwynn: Mr. Padre

____ Derek Jeter: The Yankee Kid

____ Randy Johnson: Arizona Heat!

____ Pedro Martinez: Throwing Strikes

____ Mike Piazza: Mike and the Mets

____ Alex Rodriguez: A-plus Shortstop

____ Curt Schilling: Philly Phire!

____ Sammy Sosa: Slammin' Sammy

____ Mo Vaughn: Angel on a Mission

____ Omar Vizquel:
     The Man with a Golden Glove

____ Larry Walker: Colorado Hit Man!

____ Bernie Williams: Quiet Superstar

____ Mark McGwire: Mac Attack!

Available by calling 877-424-BOOK